IN THE RHYTHM OF THE NEEDLES, THERE IS MUSIC FOR THE SOUL.

Design + Layout | Jen Geigley

The Knitting Planner

ISBN: 9781790587735
Imprint: Independently published

www.MoonPhasePublications.com

CRA015000
Crafts & Hobbies | Needlework | Knitting

10 9 8 7 6 5 4 3 2 1

this planner belongs to:

HEY!

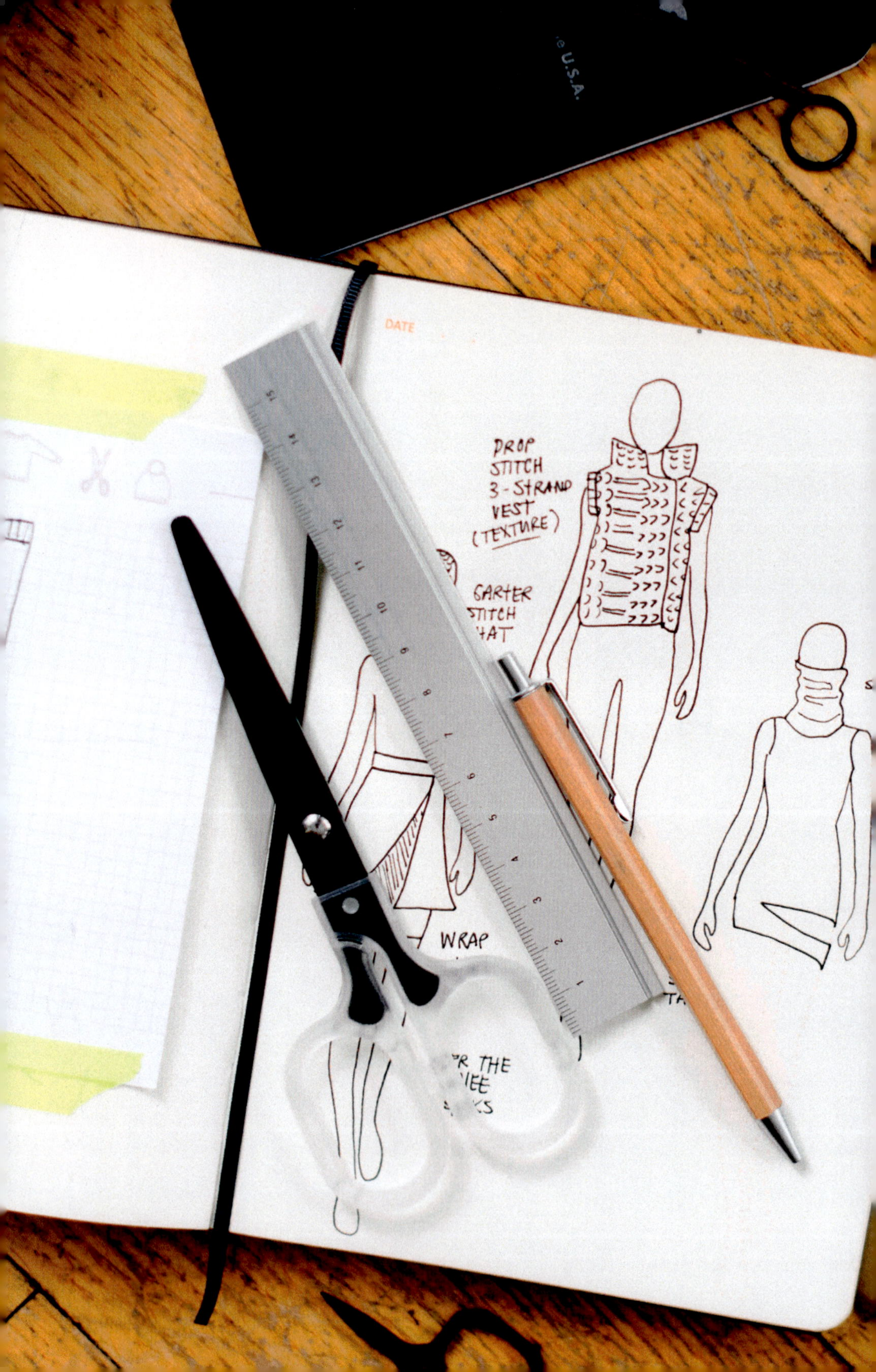
DATE
DROP
STITCH
3-STRAND
VEST
(TEXTURE)
WRAP

01

january 2019

s	m	t
30	31	1
6	7	8
13	14	15
20	21	22
27	28	29

NOTES

w	t	f	s
2	3	4	5
9	10	11	12
16	17	18	19
23	24	25	26
30	31	1	2

WEEK OF

___ /___ / ___

M

T

F

T	W
S	S

WEEK OF

___ /___ / ___

M

T

F

T

W

S

S

WEEK OF

___ /___ / ___

M

T

F

T	W
S	S

WEEK OF ___ /___ / ___	**M**
T	**F**

T

W

S

S

WEEK OF

___ /___ / ___

M

T

F

T

W

S

S

T

project

project:

notes:

planner

start date: due date:

checklist:

☐	☐
☐	☐
☐	☐
☐	☐
☐	☐
☐	☐
☐	☐
☐	☐
☐	☐
☐	☐

02

february 2019

s	m	t
27	28	29
3	4	5
10	11	12
17	18	19
24	25	26

NOTES

w	t	f	s
30	31	1	2
6	7	8	9
13	14	15	16
20	21	22	23
27	28	1	2

WEEK OF

___ /___ / ___

M

T

F

T W

S S

T

WEEK OF

___ /___ / ___

M

T

F

T

W

S

S

WEEK OF

___ /___ / ___

M

T

F

T

W

S

S

WEEK OF

___ /___ / ___

M

T

F

T W

S S

WEEK OF

___ /___ / ___

M

T

F

T	W
S	S

project

project:

notes:

planner

start date: due date:

checklist:

- [ ]
- [ ]
- [ ]
- [ ]
- [ ]
- [ ]
- [ ]
- [ ]
- [ ]
- [ ]
- [ ]
- [ ]
- [ ]
- [ ]
- [ ]
- [ ]
- [ ]
- [ ]
- [ ]
- [ ]

03

march 2019

s	m	t
24	25	26
3	4	5
10	11	12
17	18	19
24	25	26
31	1	2

NOTES

w	t	f	s
27	28	1	2
6	7	8	9
13	14	15	16
20	21	22	23
27	28	29	30
3	4	5	6

WEEK OF

___ /___ / ___

M

T

F

T

W

S

S

WEEK OF

___ /___ / ___

M

T

F

T

W

S

S

WEEK OF

___ /___ / ___

M

T

F

T	W
S	S

WEEK OF

___ /___ / ___

M

T

F

T

W

S

S

WEEK OF

___ /___ / ___

M

T

F

T

W

S

S

WEEK OF

___ /___ / ___

M

T

F

T

W

S

S

project

project:

notes:

planner

start date: due date:

checklist:

☐	☐
☐	☐
☐	☐
☐	☐
☐	☐
☐	☐
☐	☐
☐	☐
☐	☐
☐	☐

Sharpie
FIELD
NOTES
48-Page Memo Book
Durable Materials / Made in the U.S.A.

04

april 2019

s	m	t
31	1	2
7	8	9
14	15	16
21	22	23
28	29	30

NOTES

w	t	f	s
3	4	5	6
10	11	12	13
17	18	19	20
24	25	26	27
1	2	3	4

WEEK OF

___ /___ / ___

M

T

F

T

W

S

S

WEEK OF

___ /___ / ___

M

T

F

T

W

S

S

WEEK OF

___ /___ / ___

M

T

F

T

W

S

S

WEEK OF

___ /___ / ___

M

T

F

T

W

S

S

WEEK OF

___ /___ / ___

M

T

F

T W

S S

project

project:

notes:

planner

start date: due date:

checklist:

☐	☐
☐	☐
☐	☐
☐	☐
☐	☐
☐	☐
☐	☐
☐	☐
☐	☐
☐	☐

05

may 2019

s	m	t
28	29	30
5	6	7
12	13	14
19	20	21
26	27	28

NOTES

w	t	f	s
1	2	3	4
8	9	10	11
15	16	17	18
22	23	24	25
29	30	31	1

WEEK OF

___ /___ / ___

M

T

F

T

W

S

S

WEEK OF

___ /___ / ___

M

T

F

T	W
S	S

WEEK OF

___ /___ / ___

M

T

F

T

W

S

S

WEEK OF

___ /___ / ___

M

T

F

T	W
S	S

WEEK OF

___ /___ / ___

M

T

F

T

W

S

S

project

project:

notes:

planner

start date: due date:

checklist:

☐	☐
☐	☐
☐	☐
☐	☐
☐	☐
☐	☐
☐	☐
☐	☐
☐	☐
☐	☐

06

june 2019

s	m	t
26	27	28
2	3	4
9	10	11
16	17	18
23	24	25
30	1	2

NOTES

w	t	f	s
29	30	31	1
5	6	7	8
12	13	14	15
19	20	21	22
26	27	28	29
3	4	5	6

WEEK OF

___ /___ / ___

M

T

F

T	W
S	S

WEEK OF

___ /___ / ___

M

T

F

T

W

S

S

WEEK OF

___ /___ / ___

M

T

F

T

W

S

S

WEEK OF

___ /___ / ___

M

T

F

T

W

S

S

WEEK OF

___ /___ / ___

M

T

F

T	W
S	S

WEEK OF

___ /___ / ___

M

T

F

T W

S S

project

project:

notes:

planner

start date: due date:

checklist:

☐	☐
☐	☐
☐	☐
☐	☐
☐	☐
☐	☐
☐	☐
☐	☐
☐	☐
☐	☐

07

july 2019

s	m	t
30	1	2
7	8	9
14	15	16
21	22	23
28	29	30

NOTES

w	t	f	s
3	4	5	6
10	11	12	13
17	18	19	20
24	25	26	27
31	1	2	3

WEEK OF

___ /___ / ___

M

T

F

T

W

S

S

WEEK OF

___ /___ / ___

M

T

F

T	W
S	S

WEEK OF

___ /___ / ___

M

T

F

T	W
S	S

WEEK OF

___ /___ / ___

M

T

F

T	W
S	S

WEEK OF

___ /___ / ___

M

T

F

T	**W**
S	**S**

project

project:

notes:

planner

start date: due date:

checklist:

- [ ]
- [ ]
- [ ]
- [ ]
- [ ]
- [ ]
- [ ]
- [ ]
- [ ]
- [ ]
- [ ]
- [ ]
- [ ]
- [ ]
- [ ]
- [ ]
- [ ]
- [ ]
- [ ]
- [ ]

08

august 2019

s	m	t
28	29	30
4	5	6
11	12	13
18	19	20
25	26	27

NOTES

w	t	f	s
31	1	2	3
7	8	9	10
14	15	16	17
21	22	23	24
28	29	30	31

WEEK OF

___ /___ / ___

M

T

F

T	W
S	S

WEEK OF

___ /___ / ___

M

T

F

T

W

S

S

WEEK OF

___ /___ / ___

M

T

F

T	W
S	S

WEEK OF

___ /___ / ___

M

T

F

T	**W**
S	**S**

T

WEEK OF

___ /___ / ___

M

T

F

T

W

S

S

project

project:

notes:

planner

start date: due date:

checklist:

- [ ]
- [ ]
- [ ]
- [ ]
- [ ]
- [ ]
- [ ]
- [ ]
- [ ]
- [ ]
- [ ]
- [ ]
- [ ]
- [ ]
- [ ]
- [ ]
- [ ]
- [ ]
- [ ]
- [ ]

09

september 2019

s	m	t
1	2	3
8	9	10
15	16	17
22	23	24
29	30	1

NOTES

w	t	f	s
4	5	6	7
11	12	13	14
18	19	20	21
25	26	27	28
2	3	4	5

WEEK OF

___ /___ / ___

M

T

F

T	W
S	S

WEEK OF

___ /___ / ___

M

T

F

T

W

S

S

WEEK OF

___ /___ / ___

M

T

F

T

W

S

S

WEEK OF

___ /___ / ___

M

T

F

T	W
S	S

WEEK OF

___ /___ / ___

M

T

F

T W

S S

project

project:

notes:

planner

start date: due date:

checklist:

- [ ]
- [ ]
- [ ]
- [ ]
- [ ]
- [ ]
- [ ]
- [ ]
- [ ]
- [ ]
- [ ]
- [ ]
- [ ]
- [ ]
- [ ]
- [ ]
- [ ]
- [ ]
- [ ]
- [ ]

10

october 2019

s	m	t
29	30	1
6	7	8
13	14	15
20	21	22
27	28	29

NOTES

w	t	f	s
2	3	4	5
9	10	11	12
16	17	18	19
23	24	25	26
30	31	1	2

WEEK OF

___ /___ / ___

M

T

F

T

W

S

S

WEEK OF

___ /___ / ___

M

T

F

T

W

S

S

WEEK OF

___ /___ / ___

M

T

F

T

W

S

S

T

WEEK OF

___ /___ / ___

M

T

F

T	W
S	S

WEEK OF

___ /___ / ___

M

T

F

T

W

S

S

project

project:

notes:

planner

start date: due date:

checklist:

☐	☐
☐	☐
☐	☐
☐	☐
☐	☐
☐	☐
☐	☐
☐	☐
☐	☐
☐	☐

11

november 2019

s	m	t
27	28	29
3	4	5
10	11	12
17	18	19
24	25	26

NOTES

w	t	f	s
30	31	1	2
6	7	8	9
13	14	15	16
20	21	22	23
27	28	29	30

WEEK OF

___ /___ / ___

M

T

F

T

W

S

S

WEEK OF

___ /___ / ___

M

T

F

T

W

S

S

WEEK OF

___ /___ / ___

M

T

F

T

W

S

S

WEEK OF

___ /___ / ___

M

T

F

T

W

S

S

WEEK OF

___ /___ / ___

M

T

F

T	W
S	S

project

project:

notes:

planner

start date: due date:

checklist:

- [ ]
- [ ]
- [ ]
- [ ]
- [ ]
- [ ]
- [ ]
- [ ]
- [ ]
- [ ]
- [ ]
- [ ]
- [ ]
- [ ]
- [ ]
- [ ]
- [ ]
- [ ]
- [ ]
- [ ]

43.

12

december 2019

s	m	t
1	2	3
8	9	10
15	16	17
22	23	24
29	30	31

NOTES

w	t	f	s
4	5	6	7
11	12	13	14
18	19	20	21
25	26	27	28
1	2	3	4

WEEK OF

___ /___ / ___

M

T

F

T	W
S	S

WEEK OF

___ /___ / ___

M

T

F

T	**W**
S	**S**

WEEK OF

___ /___ / ___

M

T

F

T

W

S

S

WEEK OF

___ /___ / ___

M

T

F

T

W

S

S

WEEK OF

___ /___ / ___

M

T

F

T	W
S	S

project

project:

notes:

planner

start date: due date:

checklist:

- [ ]
- [ ]
- [ ]
- [ ]
- [ ]
- [ ]
- [ ]
- [ ]
- [ ]
- [ ]
- [ ]
- [ ]
- [ ]
- [ ]
- [ ]
- [ ]
- [ ]
- [ ]
- [ ]
- [ ]

A PATTERN IS ONLY A GUIDELINE.

Steven Berg

(brainstorm)

subject:

project: date:

MORE IS MORE AND LESS IS A BORE.

Stephen West

project: date:

PROPERLY PRACTICED, KNITTING SOOTHES THE TROUBLED SPIRIT, AND IT DOESN'T HURT THE UNTROUBLED SPIRIT EITHER.

Elizabeth Zimmerman

PROS/CONS

KNITTING NEEDLES
ARE YOUR
PAINTBRUSHES;
YARN IS
YOUR PAINT.

Jen Geigley

DREAMS + IDEAS

THERE ARE
NO MISTAKES,
ONLY VARIATIONS.

Steven Berg

notes

KNITTING NEEDLE CONVERSION CHART

METRIC	U.S.	U.K.
2 mm	0	14
2.25 mm	1	13
2.75 mm	2	12
3 mm	-	11
3.25 mm	3	10
3.5 mm	4	-
3.75 mm	5	9
4 mm	6	8
4.5 mm	7	7
5 mm	8	6
5.5 mm	9	5
6 mm	10	4
6.5 mm	10 1/2	3
7 mm	-	2
7.5 mm	-	1
8 mm	11	0
9 mm	13	00
10 mm	15	000
12 mm	17	-
16 mm	19	-
19 mm	35	-
25 mm	50	-

MEASUREMENTS
(myself, my family + my friends)

name ____________________
chest/bust ____________________
center back ____________________
waist ____________________
sleeve ____________________
head circumference ____________________
foot length ____________________

name ____________________
chest/bust ____________________
center back ____________________
waist ____________________
sleeve ____________________
head circumference ____________________
foot length ____________________

name ____________________
chest/bust ____________________
center back ____________________
waist ____________________
sleeve ____________________
head circumference ____________________
foot length ____________________

name ____________________
chest/bust ____________________
center back ____________________
waist ____________________
sleeve ____________________
head circumference ____________________
foot length ____________________

name ____________________
chest/bust ____________________
center back ____________________
waist ____________________
sleeve ____________________
head circumference ____________________
foot length ____________________

KNITTING PATTERN ABBREVIATIONS

alt	alternate
approx	approximately
beg	beginning
bet	between
BO	bind off
byo	backward yarn over
CC	contrasting color
cn	cable needle
CO	cast on
cont	continue
dec	decrease
dpn	double-pointed needles
foll	follow
inc	increase
k	knit
k1B	knit stitch in row below
kfb	knit 1 into front and back of a stitch; single knit increase
ksp	knit 1 stitch, slip this stitch from right needle to left needle, pass second stitch on left needle over first stitch and off left needle; return stitch to right needle; single right-leaning decrease
k2tog	knit 2 stitches together; single right-leaning decrease
kwise	knitwise
LH	left hand
lp	loop
m	marker
M1K	make one stitch knitwise; single knit increase
M1R	make one right; single right-leaning knit increase
M1L	make one left; single left-leaning knit increase
M1p	make one purlwise; single purl increase
M1rp	make one right purlwise; single right-leaning purl increase
M1lp	make one left purlwise; single left-leaning purl increase
MC	main color
p	purl
pat/patt	pattern
pfb	purl 1 into front and back of a stitch; single purl increase
pm	place marker
p2tog	purl 2 stitches together; single decrease
prev	previous
psso	pass slipped stitch over
p2sso	pass 2 slipped stitches over

pwise	purlwise
rem	remaining
rep	repeat
rev St st	reverse stockinette stitch
RH	right hand
rnd	round
RS	right side
SKP	slip 1 knitwise, knit 1, pass slip stitch over knit stitch; single left-leaning decrease
SK2P	slip 1 knitwise, knit 2 together, pass slip stitch over knit 2 together; double left-leaning decrease
sl	slip
sl1k	slip 1 knitwise
sl1p	slip 1 purlwise
sl st	slip stitch
sm	slip marker
ssk	slip 2 stitches knitwise, knit these 2 stitches together through back loops; single left-leaning decrease
ssp	slip 2 stitches knitwise, return these 2 stitches to left needle and purl them together through back loops; single left-leaning decrease
sssk	slip 3 stitches knitwise, knit these 3 stitches together through back loops; double left-leaning decrease
sssp	slip 3 stitches knitwise, return these 3 stitches to left needle and purl these 3 stitches together through back loops; double left-leaning decrease
S2KP2	slip 2 stitches as if to knit 2 together, knit 1, pass 2 slipped stitches over knit stitch; centered double decrease
SSPP2	slip 2 stitches knitwise, return these 2 stitches to left needle and then slip them as if to p2tog through back loops, purl 1, pass 2 slipped stitches over purl stitch; centered double decrease
st	stitch
St st	stockinette stitch
tbl	through back loop
tfl	through front loop
tog	together
WS	wrong side
w&t	wrap and turn
wyib	with yarn in back
wyif	with yarn in front
yb	yarn back
yfwd/yf	yarn forward
yo	yarn over
yon	yarn over needle
yrn	yarn round needle

PROJECTS I WANT TO KNIT

pattern name ______________________________
needle size ______________________________
yarn name ______________________________
yarn weight ______________________________
yardage required for my size ______________________________
gauge ______________________________
notes ______________________________

pattern name ______________________________
needle size ______________________________
yarn name ______________________________
yarn weight ______________________________
yardage required for my size ______________________________
gauge ______________________________
notes ______________________________

pattern name ______________________________
needle size ______________________________
yarn name ______________________________
yarn weight ______________________________
yardage required for my size ______________________________
gauge ______________________________
notes ______________________________

PROJECTS I WANT TO KNIT

pattern name ____________________
needle size ____________________
yarn name ____________________
yarn weight ____________________
yardage required for my size ____________________
gauge ____________________
notes ____________________

pattern name ____________________
needle size ____________________
yarn name ____________________
yarn weight ____________________
yardage required for my size ____________________
gauge ____________________
notes ____________________

pattern name ____________________
needle size ____________________
yarn name ____________________
yarn weight ____________________
yardage required for my size ____________________
gauge ____________________
notes ____________________

PROJECTS I WANT TO KNIT

pattern name ______________________________
needle size ______________________________
yarn name ______________________________
yarn weight ______________________________
yardage required for my size ______________________________
gauge ______________________________
notes ______________________________

____
____
____
____

pattern name ______________________________
needle size ______________________________
yarn name ______________________________
yarn weight ______________________________
yardage required for my size ______________________________
gauge ______________________________
notes ______________________________

____
____
____
____

pattern name ______________________________
needle size ______________________________
yarn name ______________________________
yarn weight ______________________________
yardage required for my size ______________________________
gauge ______________________________
notes ______________________________

____
____
____
____

KNITTER'S GRAPH PAPER

KNITTER'S GRAPH PAPER

NOTES

NOTES

NOTES

KNIT ON, WITH CONFIDENCE AND HOPE, THROUGH ALL CRISIS.

Elizabeth Zimmerman

49905556R10131

Made in the USA
Columbia, SC
29 January 2019